CW01095739

Picture Credits

t=top b=bottom c=centre l=left r=right m=middle

Front Cover Images: doctorbass/Shutterstock, Isselee/Dreamstime, Miguelangel pallardodelrio/Shutterstock, Rm/Shutterstock

Back Cover Images: USAsearch.gov, Glengaffney/Shutterstock, Emanon/dreamstime

Border Images: Kenm/Dreamstime, sandybuckley/istock, Djmattaar/Shutterstock, sandybuckley/istock, Uniqueglen/Dreamstime.

Insides: RichardFitzer/Shutterstock: 6-7, q2amediaimagebank, Wes Eplen/US. Navy: 7b, Noaa: 8c, Hwinther/Dreamstime: 8-9, SashaDavas/Shutterstock: 9b, usasearch.gov: 10t, adwalsh/istock: 12t, Kenm/dreamstime: 13t, glengaffney/Shutterstock: 14b, Kenm/Dreamstime: 15t, Emanon/Dreamstime: 16, Isselee/Dreamstime: 17, Frigjalk/dreamstime: 19t, Cfikker/Dreamstime: 21t, Isselee/Dreamstime: 22b, sethakan/istock: 23mt, MiguelAngelPallardodelRio/Shutterstock: 23b, Jandaly/Dreamstime: 24, eric martinez/Fotolia: 25t, Baddpix/istock: 26, Isselee/Dreamstime: 27t, DJ Mattaar/shutterstock: 28b, Nj/fotolia: 28-29, Kenm/Dreamstime: 29b, Hatch/istock: 30, doctorbass/shutterstock: 31t, MichaelVigliotti/shutterstock: 31b, Kenm/Dreamstime: 32-33, Margaret Brudnicka/shutterstock: 33b, sandybuckley/istock: 34, John Solie/Shutterstock: 36t, Ovidiulordachi/shutterstock: 36-37, Taolmor/shutterstock: 37t, add2007/istock: 40, Flory/istock: 41b

ALL ILLUSTRATIONS MADE BY Q2A MEDIA

Copyright: North Parade Publishing Ltd.
Published By: North Parade Publishing Ltd.
4 North Parade, BA1 1LF, UK

First Published: 2008

All rights reserved. No part of this publication may be reprinted, stored in a retrieval system or transmitted, in any form or by any means, electronic, mechanical, photocopying, recording, or otherwise, without the prior permission of the copyright holder.

Designed and packaged by
Q2AMEDIA
Printed in China.

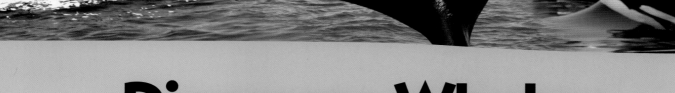

Discover Whales

Contents

Under the Sea

Whales are warm-blooded underwater mammals that can be found all over the world.

Where Do They Come From?

Whales belong to the order Cetacea and are descended from land mammals that belonged to the order Artiodactyl, or even-toed ungulates. It is believed that they first ventured into the waters about 50 million years ago. The Basilosaurus and Dorudon were fully aquatic creatures recognisable as whales.

What Do They Look Like?

Whales are warm-blooded sea mammals that breathe through lungs rather than gills. They are usually black, grey, tan or white in colour. A thick layer of fat, known as blubber, underlies the inside of their skin. There are two main types of whales, Baleen and Toothed.

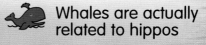 Whales are actually related to hippos

Fun Fact

Hind limbs have disappeared in whales due to evolution, but many whales still retain remnants of their forelimbs.

Are They In Danger?

Whales have very few natural predators. In fact, humans pose the greatest threat to their survival. For centuries, whales have been hunted for their meat, bone, blubber and oil. This is known as whaling and has resulted in a widespread decline in their numbers. Harmful human activities, like the contamination of the oceans with toxins and industrial waste, as well as the use of sonar by ships and submarines, put whales and other sea creatures in danger.

The tail fins, or flukes, help the whales to move in water

Many modern ships use sonar to navigate, which is thought to be harmful to whales

Mammals

Although whales look like fish, they are actually mammals and have distinct mammal-like features.

 Whales have tiny bristles around their mouths that help them to feel things

Mammal Features

All whales are warm-blooded mammals. This means that they produce and regulate their own heat in their body. Whales also breathe through their lungs with the help of blowholes located at the top of their heads. Like land mammals, female whales give birth to live young and nurse them on milk until they can feed for themselves.

 Beluga whales have a heart rate of 12-20 beats per minute

Echolocation

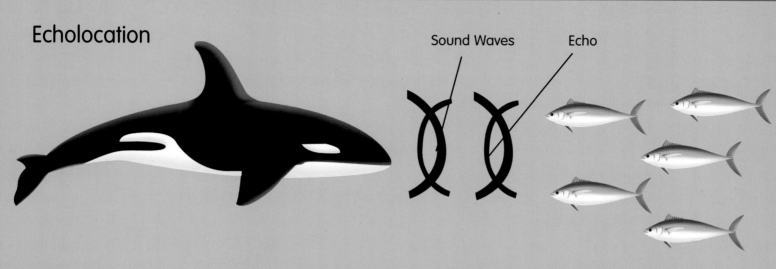

Sound Waves   Echo

 Whales use echolocation to find their way underwater. They also use it to detect predators, prey and any other kind of danger that may lie ahead of them

Echolocation

Whales possess a highly developed sense of hearing. In this they are aided by their ability to echolocate. Echolocation is a complex process in which whales emit clicking sounds which are channeled by a fat-filled, melon-shaped organ in their head. The sound bounces off an object and comes back to the whale in the form of an echo. Whales receive this sound in a cavity full of fat in their lower jaw. From there it is sent to the brain. Echolocation helps whales to understand the shape, distance, texture and location of different objects.

Fun Fact

Echolocation is better developed in Toothed whales than in Baleen whales.

Magnetic Personality

Whales possess another special ability. It is believed that they can detect the magnetic field of the Earth and use this to navigate during long migrations. It is, however, not clear how they are able to do this. Some scientists believe that when whales become stranded on beaches it is because an abnormality the Earth's magnetic field has drawn them there.

Whale Sounds

The sounds made by whales, in order to communicate and for other purposes, are known as whale song.

The most haunting sounds are made by Humpack whales

Why Do They Sing?

The sense of hearing is very important to whales because they depend on it for almost all their daily activities. This is mainly because their other senses are not as effective underwater as sound. Whales use sound for communication, echolocation and navigation. It also helps them to detect the depth of water and the shape and size of an obstacle.

Toothed Whales

Toothed whales have a more complex system of sound production than Baleen whales. High-frequency clicks and whistles are produced through a narrow passage in their head known as the phonic lips. Air passing through here causes the tissues to vibrate, producing a sound. Most whales have two sets of phonic lips and can produce two different sounds.

Baleen Whales

Unlike Toothed whales, Baleen whales do not possess phonic lips. The larynx is used instead, much the same as humans, but the mechanism is not exactly like ours. They probably recycle air within their bodies to produce sound. There is still no clear information on their sound-producing mechanism.

Fun Fact

Toothed whales produce sounds that range between 10-31,000 Hz.

 Baleen whales use their larynx to produce sound

 Sound producing mechanism in Dolphins and Toothed whales

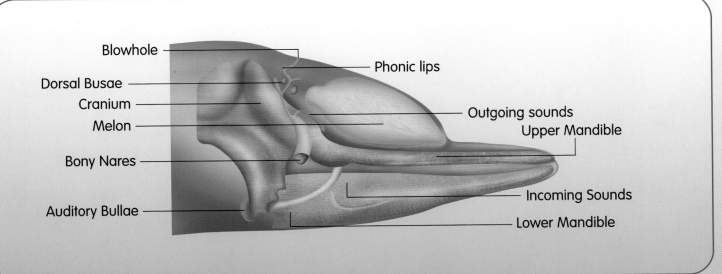

Blowhole

Dorsal Busae

Cranium

Melon

Bony Nares

Auditory Bullae

Phonic lips

Outgoing sounds

Upper Mandible

Incoming Sounds

Lower Mandible

No Sleep

Like all mammals, whales need sleep and they have specially adapted their sleeping habits to suit their environment.

Why Can't They Sleep?

Whales have a respiratory system that is quite different from land mammals. It is not an involuntary action. Instead, they actually breathe at will. Moreover, because they live underwater, they must keep moving at all times to prevent themselves from sinking to the bottom of the sea. As a result, whales cannot reach a deep sleep, otherwise they would drown!

 Whales need to keep swimming so that they do not sink to the bottom

Beauty Sleep

Their inabilty to sleep deeply does not mean that whales do not sleep at all. In fact, they require 8 hours of sleep each day. They are able to do so by letting only one part of their brain sleep while keeping the other part awake. It is believed that some Toothed whales actually sleep in large groups, where one member stays completely awake, and has the task of reminding the others to breathe.

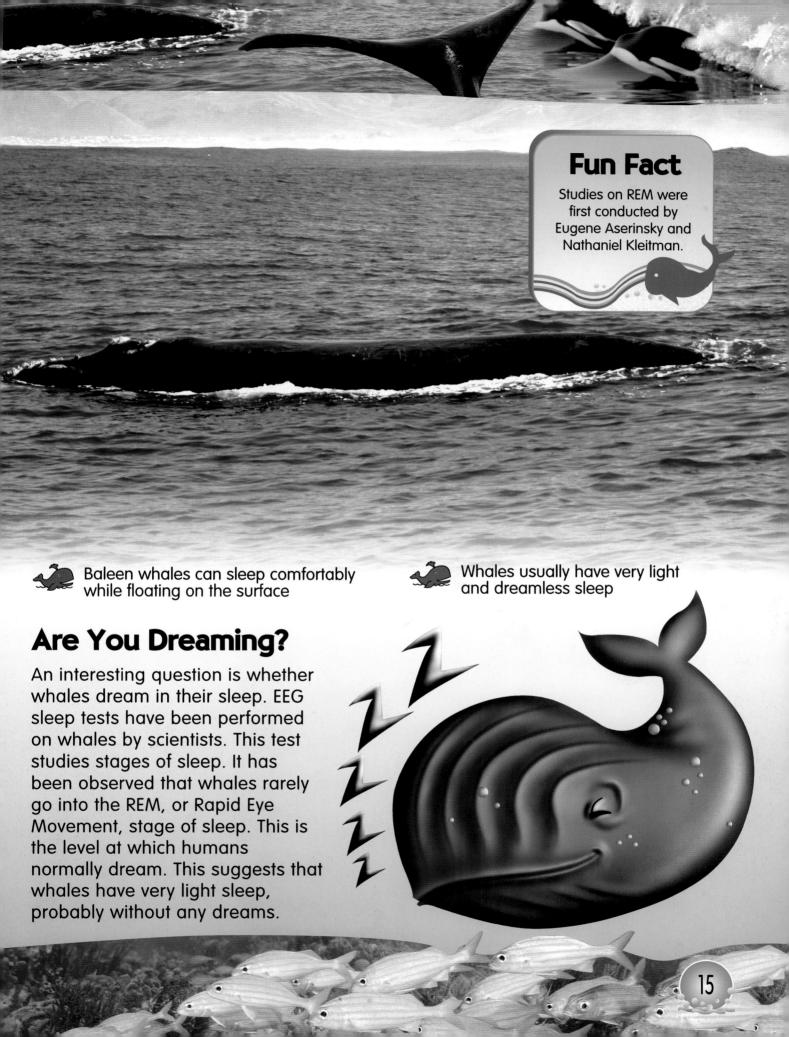

Fun Fact

Studies on REM were first conducted by Eugene Aserinsky and Nathaniel Kleitman.

Baleen whales can sleep comfortably while floating on the surface

Whales usually have very light and dreamless sleep

Are You Dreaming?

An interesting question is whether whales dream in their sleep. EEG sleep tests have been performed on whales by scientists. This test studies stages of sleep. It has been observed that whales rarely go into the REM, or Rapid Eye Movement, stage of sleep. This is the level at which humans normally dream. This suggests that whales have very light sleep, probably without any dreams.

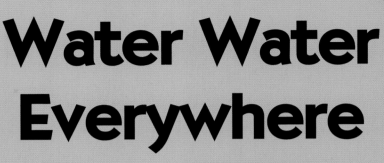

Water Water Everywhere

A long time ago whales, dolphins and porpoises were land animals. Over the course of millions of years they adapted themselves to live underwater.

Body of A Swimmer

Whales have many special features that are well adapted for swimming underwater. Their bodies are streamlined in order to reduce friction with the water. They have very little hair on them, which also reduces friction. Whales have very flexible rib cages that, in some cases, are completely free and unattached from the spinal column. This enables the chest to open out wide and let in more air while breathing.

 Whales have specially designed bone structures that help them to swim

 Whales have streamlined bodies to reduce friction with the water

Powerful Necks

Whales have very powerful necks that allow them to thrust through the water at great speed. Their special bone structure helps them to do this. The vertebrae in their necks are short and partially joined into a single mass of bones. This provides them with great strength. Also, the bones that connect the neck vertebrae are reduced in numbers, which give them more flexibility underwater.

Fun Fact

Some whales still possess remnants of a pelvis.

Flukes and Flippers

Whales use the horizontal flukes in their tails to propel themselves through the water. Flippers are used for steering. These are made up of short and flat arm bones, several elongated fingers and disc-like wrist bones. The joint at their elbow is almost fixed in one place, making their flippers rigid. All these features help them to swim efficiently.

Whales have almost rigid flippers, that help them to steer in water

Heat Regulation

The world's oceans can be extremely cold, which is why whales have to be well protected in order to keep themselves warm.

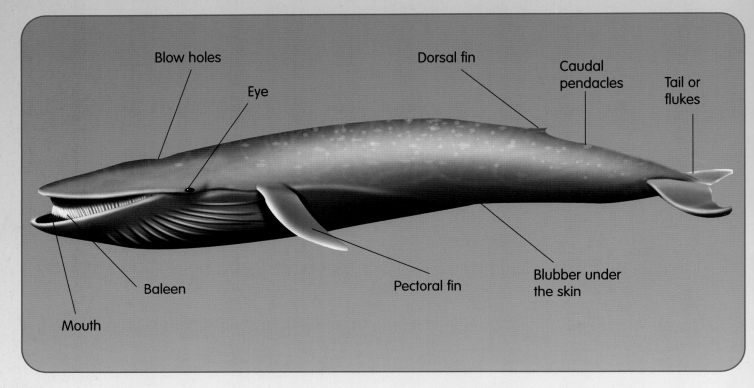

Blow holes

Eye

Dorsal fin

Caudal pendacles

Tail or flukes

Baleen

Mouth

Pectoral fin

Blubber under the skin

 The blubber is a layer of fat under the skin

Effective Insulation

The most effective protection against the cold that whales have is their blubber. This is a thick layer of fat found under the skin. It runs across their whole body except for their flippers and flukes. The blubber acts as an insulatory layer, which prevents body heat from escaping, conserving heat. Blubber is also used to store energy for when food is scarce.

Fun Fact

Heat is lost in water around 27 times faster than in air under similar temperatures.

Many sea mammals, such as sea otters, have fur instead of blubber

Why Is Blubber Better Than Fur?

Blubber is better at conserving heat than fur. Pockets of air are held by fur and this traps heat. However, when brought under pressure these pockets of air can be released. Blubber retains its level of insulation under pressure.

Whale limbs are small, which helps reduce heat loss

Others Methods of Conserving Heat

The fusiform (tapered at both ends) shape of their body and small sized limbs, minimises the surface area of the whale's extremeties, where the majority of heat is lost, and helps reduce the loss of body heat. Moreover, the whale's circulatory system also helps to regulate body heat by either keeping in or letting out body heat, when necessary.

Feeding Time

There are two types of whales – Toothed and Baleen – and each type has a different method of feeding.

Filtering Food

Baleen whales are different because they have no teeth. Instead of teeth they have baleen plates, which act like sieves to filter food from the water. Baleen whales have two blowholes, from which, water blows out in a v-shape. The females of the species are usually larger than the males and they are all generally much bigger in size than Toothed whales.

Fun Fact

Sperm whales do not use their teeth to feed. Instead they use them to show anger and for show!

Baleen whales use the baleen plates in their mouth to filter their food

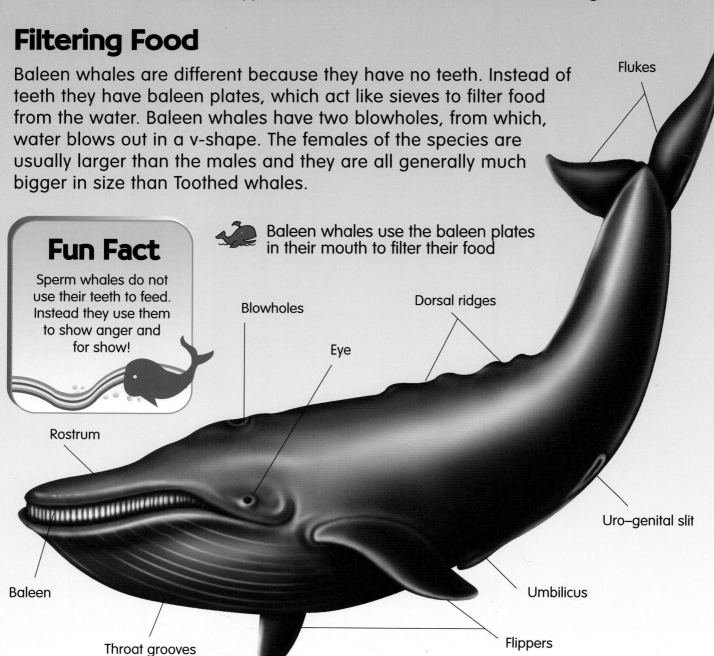

Flukes

Blowholes

Eye

Dorsal ridges

Rostrum

Uro–genital slit

Baleen

Umbilicus

Throat grooves

Flippers

Sinking their Teeth in

Toothed whales are distinguished from Baleen whales by their teeth. These whales are smaller in size and have a single blowhole instead of two. They also have a melon shaped organ on their heads, which has been evolved for echolocation. These whales do not have any vocal cords. Sound is produced by them through their blowholes. They also do not possess any sense of smell or saliva glands. Toothed whales are good hunters. They use their teeth to hold on to their prey. They usually feed on squid, fish and small marine mammals.

 Toothed whales have many small conical teeth to catch their prey

 Grey whales increase their body weight 16–30% during the feeding season

Time To Eat!

Most whales have a feeding season. Food intake during the feeding season is high, with excess energy being stored as blubber. This blubber sustains the whale during the winter months. Baleen whales spend about four to six months in the summer feeding intensively and the following six to eight months are spent travelling and breeding. During these months they eat much less, if at all.

21

Deep Breaths

Whales are sea-living mammals and like all mammals breathe oxygen into their lungs, rather than filtering oxygen through gills, like fish.

Blowholes

Whales breathe through their nostrils, which are known as blowholes. These are usually located on the top of their heads and are connected to their lungs through the trachea. Muscular flaps cover the blowholes, which prevent water from entering when submerged and just before a deep dive the strong muscles around the blowholes relax and the flap is allowed to cover them. Sperm whales are known to dive as deep as 9186 ft (2,800 m) for more than 2 hours at a time!

 The blowholes on top of the head allow it to breathe air from the surface

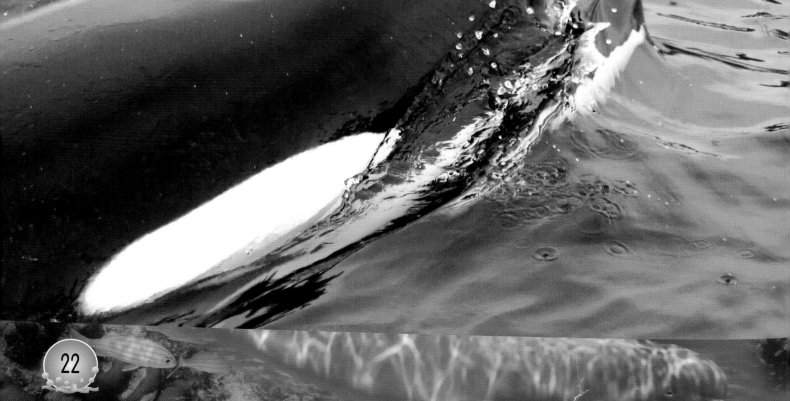

Breathing In and Out

Respiration is not controlled by their autonomic nervous system, but is an act of will for whales which helps them remain underwater for long periods. When whales need air they surface and first blow out the stale air, which is when misty vapour is seen gushing out of the blowholes. They then breathe in fresh air just before diving. The air passes to the lungs, and from there oxygen is carried to the other parts of their body by their blood.

Fun Fact

Unlike humans, whales cannot breathe through their mouths.

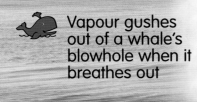
Vapour gushes out of a whale's blowhole when it breathes out

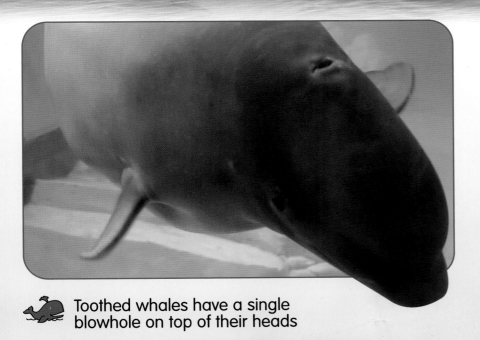
Toothed whales have a single blowhole on top of their heads

How Many Blowholes?

Whales breathe through their blowholes, located at the top of their head. Some whales have one blowhole, while others have two. Most Baleen whales possess two blowholes while Toothed whales usually have just one. This is because in Baleen whales the second blowhole evolved through time to help in echolocation.

Mother Dear

All whales are viviparous mammals, meaning the mother gives birth to the young and nurtures them with her milk.

Whales protect and care for their young ones for a long period of time

Birth

Whales give birth to their young, which are known as calves. Mothers tend to give birth seasonally, and normally a single calf is born every 1–3 years. They prefer giving birth in warm tropical waters and the birth of twins has been known, but is very rare. A whale's gestation period lasts between 9 and 18 months, depending on species.

Fun Fact

Killer Whales, or Orcas, have a gestation period of over 16 months.

Young Whales

Newborn whales can swim almost immediately after birth and straight after birth their natural instinct is to head up to the surface of the water to breathe. Calves usually feed on their mother's milk and some whales are known to nurse their offspring for up to a year. Young whales often have a mottled colouration as camouflage, protecting them from predators. Newborn whales can have a light covering of hair, but this is usually lost as they grow older.

Whale calves are born with open eyes and alert senses. They swim up to the surface immediately after birth to breathe

Big and Blue

Blue whales give birth to the largest young of any creature in the world. These huge babies are usually around 7.6 m (25 ft) in length and 5.4–7.3 tonnes (6–8 tons) in weight. The Blue whale's gestation period lasts between 11–12 months, and they give birth every 2–3 years. Baby Blue whales are fed up to 200 litres (50 gallons) of milk every day and they gain about 44 kg (100 lbs) in weight daily!

 The milk of the female Blue whale is very rich in fat

Types of Whales

All whales belong to the order Cetacea. As we've discovered, there are two main types of whales – Baleen and Toothed.

Baleen Whales

Baleen whales seive their food from the water. Baleen whales make up the Mysticeti suborder of Cetacea. For such enormous creatures, a Baleen whale's diet is actually composed of tiny creatures. They feed mainly on krill, which are shrimp-like crustaceans and are consumed in vast quantities.

Fun Fact

Blue whales have 320 pairs of baleen plates and dark grey bristles.

 Baleen whales are usually larger in size than Toothed whales

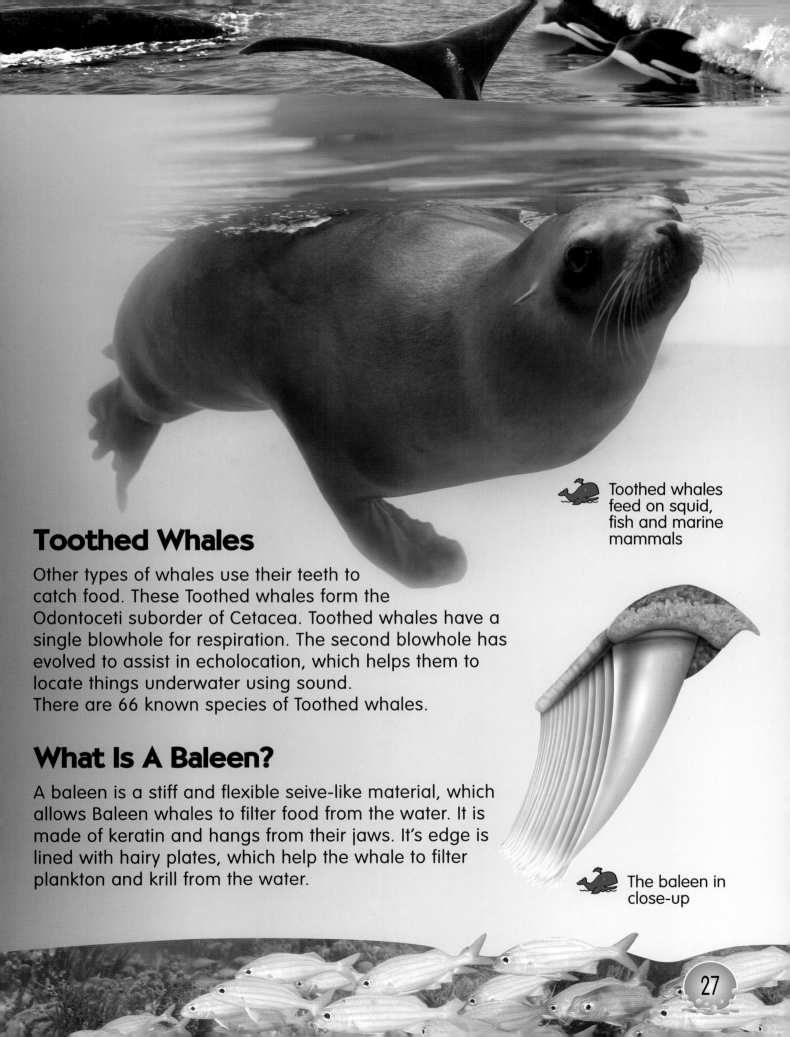

Toothed Whales

Other types of whales use their teeth to catch food. These Toothed whales form the Odontoceti suborder of Cetacea. Toothed whales have a single blowhole for respiration. The second blowhole has evolved to assist in echolocation, which helps them to locate things underwater using sound.
There are 66 known species of Toothed whales.

What Is A Baleen?

A baleen is a stiff and flexible seive-like material, which allows Baleen whales to filter food from the water. It is made of keratin and hangs from their jaws. It's edge is lined with hairy plates, which help the whale to filter plankton and krill from the water.

Toothed whales feed on squid, fish and marine mammals

The baleen in close-up

The Baleen Family

The Mysticeti suborder of Baleen whales contains four families and fourteen species of whales.

What Are They?

Baleen whales are some of the largest animals on Earth. Not all Baleen whales feed in the same way. There are some that swim and gulp food. Others keep their mouths open at all times and food filters through. Some whales do both. Another technique of feeding is known as benthic feeding, which means they find their food in the silt of the sea bed.

Humpback whales have white patches on their undersides

Baleen whales feed on different types of fish, krill and plankton

Fun Fact

Right whales may have as many as 100 tiny hairs on their upper jaws and around 300 on their lower jaws.

Humpback Whales

One of the most impressive Baleen whales is the Humpback. They are known for the beautiful and haunting songs they produce and their complex system of feeding. Humpback whales can dive for as long as 30 minutes. They get their name from the stance they take while diving. Most Humpback whales live for around 45-50 years.

I Am Right

Right whales have lower jaws that look like bows and very big heads. Little is known about them, but it is believed that they live for over 60 years. The people who traditionally hunted these creatures thought that they were the 'right', or correct, whales to hunt because of the amount of blubber they contained. This is where their name comes from.

Right whales are black or dark grey in colour with patches of either brown or white, or both

Toothy Smiles

Toothed whales form a suborder of Cetaceans called Odontoceti and are characterised by their teeth and the hunting of prey.

Look At My Teeth

Toothed whales are different from Baleen whales mainly because they have teeth to catch their food. However, they cannot use their peg-shaped teeth to chew their food. Some species of Toothed whales have as many as 250 teeth, while others may only have two!

Toothed whales use their teeth to catch food such as squid, fish and marine mammals

Sperm Whales

Sperm whales are the largest among all Toothed whales. They may grow to a length of around 17–20 m (50–60 ft) and weigh 36–45 tonnes (40–50 tons). They also have the largest head of all animals, which houses a very big brain that may weigh as much as 9 kg (20 lbs). Sperm whales are protected by a covering of spermaceti oil produced by an organ located in their head. They can live for more than 70 years.

Fun Fact

Sperm whales are often found logging. This is where they lie still on the surface with their tail hanging down.

 Sperm whales are the largest Toothed whales and cannot move very fast because of their huge bulk

Narwhals

Narwhals are fascinating Toothed whales, best known for the single long tooth that the males possess. These whales are found in the icy Arctic region, but are very rarely seen. As a result, very little is known about them, which adds to their mystery. Male narwhals have two teeth in their upper jaw. The left tooth grows long, and is usually twisted and hollow inside. They are probably meant for protection. Narwhals usually travel in pods of 4–20 whales, and feed mainly on shrimp, squid and small marine mammals.

 The single long tooth of a narwhal can grow to 3 m (10 ft) in length!

Feeling Blue

The largest and loudest animal on Earth is the Blue whale.

We Are Big

Female Blue whales are usually larger in size than males. On average they grow to a length of 25 m (80 ft) and weigh about 109 tonnes (120 tons). The largest Blue whale ever measured was 29 m (94 ft) in length and weighed 158 tonnes (174 tons)! Blue whales also have huge hearts that weigh around 450 kg (1,000 lbs).

 Blue whales are much larger in size than any other creature that lives underwater

How Do I Look?

Blue whales are huge Baleen whales that have two blowholes and a thick layer of blubber. They are usually blue-grey in colour and have grooves in their throats which allow them to expand while feeding. These huge whales have yellow, grey or brown patches on their underbelly. Their dorsal fins are small and sickle-shaped and found near their tail. The Blue whale's blood alone weighs 6,400 kg (14,000 lbs).

 Blue whales have flippers that measure 2.4 m (8 ft) in length and 7.6 m (25 ft) in width

Fun Fact

Blue whale calls are extremely loud and can reach a level of 188 decibels, compared to humans which can only manage about 70 decibles.

What's Cooking?

Blue whales are carnivores that feed on small fish, plankton and tiny crustaceans such as krill with the help of their baleen plates. They are gulpers – that is, they take a gulp of water and then filter the water out, retaining any food it contained. Around 320 pairs of black baleen plates are present in their upper jaws that have dark grey bristles at the edge. Blue whales also have huge tongues, which weigh a staggering 3.8 tonnes (4 tons)! A Blue whale of average size may eat up to 4,100 kg (9,000 lbs) of food daily. That is a lot of food!

Blue whales feed on large amounts of krill, plankton, other tiny crustaceans and small fish

Summer Holiday

Whales are known to migrate thousands of miles every year to feed and give birth to their calves.

Whales carry out seasonal migrations every year. They usually travel together

Time To Go

Whales, like most Cetaceans, follow seasonal migration. Baleen whales are known for their particularly long migration routes. Most whales travel in small groups or pods and move to cold-water areas for feeding and warm-water regions for giving birth to their young.

Fun Fact

Adult Humpback whales do not feed during the winter months. Instead, they live off their layer of fat, called blubber.

A Long Long Way

The longest migration route of any whale is undertaken by the Grey whale. They cover a huge distance of 19,312 km (12,000 miles) in a single trip, to and from their destination. In October they start migrating from the feeding grounds at the Chukchi and Bering seas, southwards to their calving grounds in Baja California, Mexico. They remain there for another 2-3 months, after which they return to their feeding grounds.

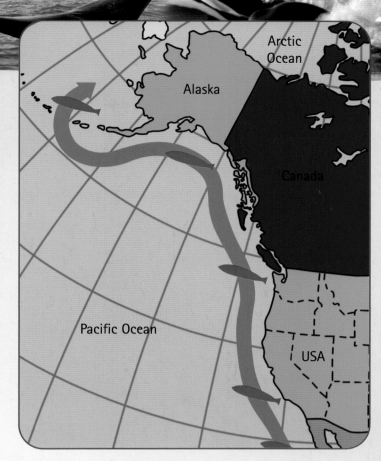

 Grey whales carry out the longest migrations among all whales. The migration takes several months

Humpback Migration

Humpback whales also travel a long distance during their seasonal migration, covering about 6,437 km (4,000 miles) each way. They give birth to their calves in warm tropical waters during the winter months and then migrate to the cold Polar regions to feed during summer. These whales usually do not take much rest during their long journeys. They are also capable of swimming quite quickly, reaching speeds of about 14 km/h (9 mph) at times.

 Humpback whales migrate along the eastern coast of North America

In Books and Culture

Numerous references are made to whales in both classical and popular literature. They are also associated with divinity in many cultures.

Holy References

References to whales are found in the Holy Bible. The King James version of the Holy Bible speaks about whales in four different places. In the book of Genesis, it mentions how God created the great whales. The Prophet Jonah was said to have been swallowed by a whale. This reference is also made in the Qur'an, the central religious text of Islam.

The Holy Bible has as many as four references to whales

The Sea of Marmara

Divine Whales

In parts of Vietnam and Ghana, whales are considered holy. They have been known to hold funerals for dead whales found on the beach - a custom that has been inherited from Vietnam's early sea-based Austro-Asiatic culture. Whales are celebrated through songs, art and whale watching in many parts of the world, such as Kodiak Alaska and Sitka.

Vietnamese fishermen sometimes hold funerals for dead whales

In Literature

Whales have been mentioned in literature many times. The Old English poem *Beowulf* describes the sea as a 'whale-road'. Procopius of Caesarea, an important Eastern Roman scholar, spoke about a whale who destroyed fisheries in the Sea of Marmara. Then, of course, there is the American novel *Moby-Dick,* about a whaling boat's seach for a Sperm whale.

Fun Fact

The word 'whale' is no longer used in the New International Version of the Christian Bible.

No Longer Around

Whales evolved over millions of years, from land-living creatures the size of modern wolves, to water-living mammals that breathe through their blowholes.

Pakicetus

One of the earliest ancestors of modern day whales was the Pakicetus. These now extinct creatures, roamed the Earth during the early Eocene period, millions of years ago. Their fossils have been found in Pakistan, hence their name, in an area that was once a part of the ancient Tethys Sea coastline. These early 'whales' were completely land-living, about the same size as wolves, and looked very much like another now extinct creature, called the Mesonychid.

Ambulocetus

The Ambulocetus or 'walking whales' were some of the earliest whales that roamed the Earth. These ancient creatures could move on land as well as in water, and their fossils are very important in the study of whale evolution from land-living mammals to water-living ones. Their teeth show that they could survive in both fresh and salt waters.

 Skeletons of the Pakicetus were first discovered in 2001 in Pakistan

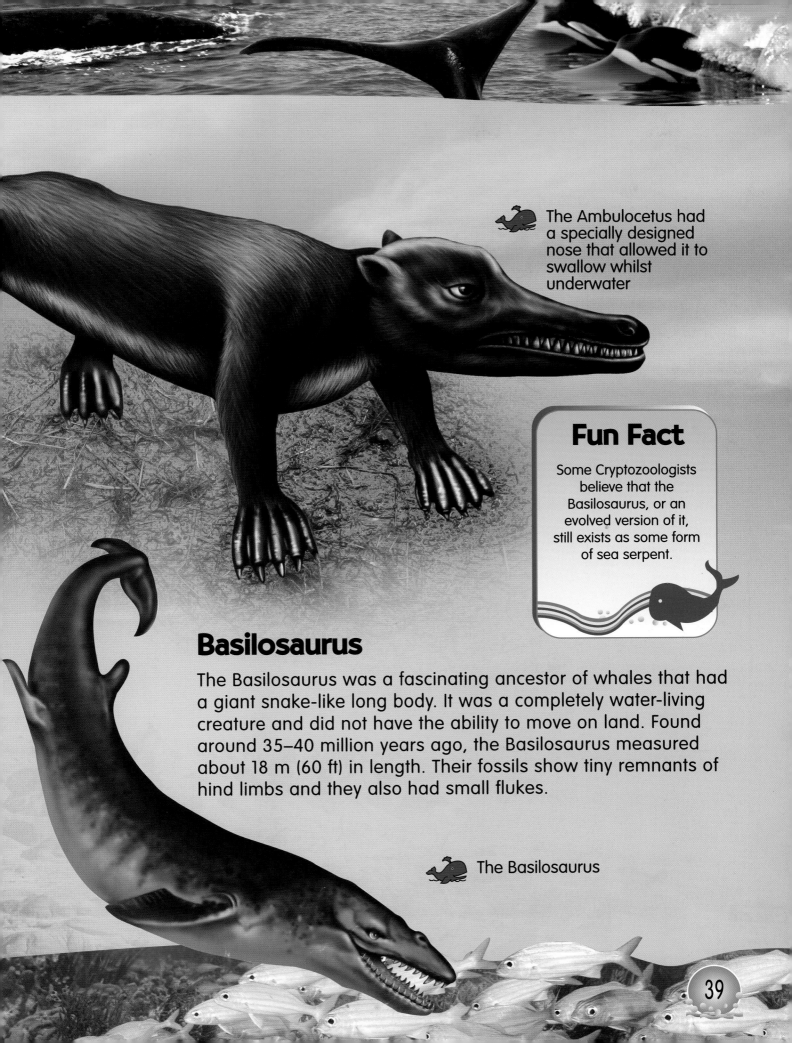

The Ambulocetus had a specially designed nose that allowed it to swallow whilst underwater

Fun Fact

Some Cryptozoologists believe that the Basilosaurus, or an evolved version of it, still exists as some form of sea serpent.

Basilosaurus

The Basilosaurus was a fascinating ancestor of whales that had a giant snake-like long body. It was a completely water-living creature and did not have the ability to move on land. Found around 35–40 million years ago, the Basilosaurus measured about 18 m (60 ft) in length. Their fossils show tiny remnants of hind limbs and they also had small flukes.

The Basilosaurus

In Danger

The greatest threat to whales comes from us – humans!
Activities such as whaling have greatly depleted their numbers.

Hunted

For centuries whales have been hunted for their meat, baleen plates, blubber and oil. This activity is known as whaling and was extensively practised during the 19th and 20th centuries greatly reducing the number of whales. As a result, whaling has now been banned in several countries to protect their numbers. However, some countries, such as Japan, Iceland and Norway, still allow whaling, despite international condemnation.

Fun Fact

Toxic chemicals have been found to cause loss of hearing in whales.

Many whale deaths are caused by accident as bycatch, where they become trapped in trawler nets

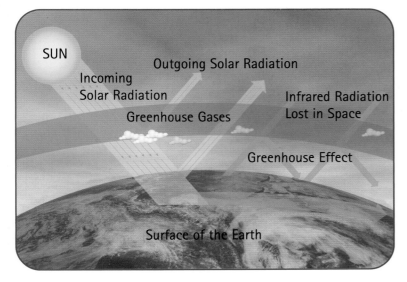

SUN

Incoming Solar Radiation

Outgoing Solar Radiation

Greenhouse Gases

Infrared Radiation Lost in Space

Greenhouse Effect

Surface of the Earth

 Global warming is raising the temperature of the world and affecting the conditions that are necessary for the survival of whales

The Environment

Environmental issues, such as global warming and climate change, are affecting whale numbers. The warming of the waters is killing krill, which is the main source of food for many whales. Moreover, Seismic testing, which is used to find gas and oil, is very harmful as it affects the hearing and echolocation abilities of whales.

The Human Factor

Harmful human practises cause the greatest damage to whale populations around the world. Dumping of dangerous toxins in and around the waters where whales live is destroying their habitats. Careless fishing and accidents with ships are also responsible for their depleting numbers.

 Litter pollutes the seas and is washed up on our beaches

Facts at a Glance

🐋 Blue whales are the largest animals in the world. They can grow to a length equivalent to the height of a 9-storey building!

🐋 Dwarf Sperm whales are the smallest whales. Adults measure around 2.6 m (8.5 ft) in length.

🐋 Shortfin Pilot whales are the fastest swimming whales. They can reach a speed of 48 km/h (30 mph).

🐋 Grey whales migrate the longest distance, covering about 1,9312 km (12,000 miles) every year.

🐋 The largest brain in the animal world belongs to the Sperm whale.

🐋 When Right whales die their bodies float on the surface.

- Humpback whales are sometimes called 'singing' whales.

- Fin whales use their flukes as weapons when defending themselves.

- The most endangered whale in the ocean is the Northern Right whale.

- Right whales have the longest baleen among all whales.

- Right whales also make the lowest frequency sound of any whale, at 3–5 Hz.

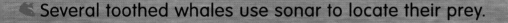

- Whales and hippos are closely related.

- It is believed that narwhals gave rise to the legend of the unicorns.

- In each mouthful, a Blue whales takes in equal to around 256,000 glasses of water, which is then expelled through the baleen plates.

- Several toothed whales use sonar to locate their prey.

Glossary

Camouflage: The ability in animals to merge with their surroundings so that they cannot be distinguished from the things around them.

Circulatory system: A system in the body of an animal which regulates the flow of blood to and from the cells, and transports nutrients, gases and water throughout the body.

Cryptozoologist: A group of people who look for proof of the existence of creatures that are rumoured to exist, such as the Loch Ness monster.

Fossil: Any part or impression of the body of an animal or plant that existed a long time ago, such as footprints or the skeleton.

Fusiform: Refers to a body which is narrow or tapering at its two ends.

Global warming: The increase in the average temperature of the air near the Earth's surface, particularly in recent years.

Insulation: The prevention of loss of heat, sound or electricity into the surrounding area.

Larynx: An organ in animals in which the vocal cords and other vocal organs lie.

Mammal: Warm-blooded animals that share common features, such as giving birth to live young and nursing them.

Mottled: Blotches or spots in the colouring of a body.

Navigate: To move or find one's way.

Predator: An animal that hunts other animals for food.

Streamline: Designed in such a way that it offers the least resistance to either air or water.

Tissue: A group of cells in the body of an animal or plant that comprise its make-up.

Toxin: A poisonous substance usually produced by living organisms.

Vibrate: Continuous and rapid movement to and fro.

Index